Super Cats

True Stories of Felines That Made History

Elizabeth MacLeod

annick press
toronto + berkeley

We acknowledge the support of the Canada Council for the Arts and the Ontario Arts Council, and the participation of the Government of Canada/la participation du gouvernement du Canada for our publishing activities.

ONTARIO ARTS COUNCIL
CONSEIL DES ARTS DE L'ONTARIO
an Ontario government agency
un organisme du gouvernement de l'Ontario

Canadä

Cataloging in Publication

MacLeod, Elizabeth, author
　　　　Super cats : true stories of felines that made history / Elizabeth MacLeod.
Issued in print and electronic formats.
ISBN 978-1-55451-994-1 (hardcover).--ISBN 978-1-55451-993-4 (softcover).--
ISBN 978-1-55451-996-5 (PDF).--ISBN 978-1-55451-995-8 (EPUB)
　　　　1. Cats--Juvenile literature. 2. Cats--History--Juvenile literature.
3. Cats--Miscellanea--Juvenile literature. I. Title.
SF445.7.M3 2017　　　　　　　　　j636.8　　　　　　　　　C2017-905810-X
　　　　　　　　　　　　　　　　　　　　　　　　　　　　　　　　C2017-905811-8

Published in the U.S.A. by Annick Press (U.S.) Ltd.
Distributed in Canada by University of Toronto Press.
Distributed in the U.S.A. by Publishers Group West.

Printed in China

www.annickpress.com

Also available in e-book format. Please visit
www.annickpress.com/ebooks.html for more details.

With lots of love to those purr-fect cats
Percy, Poppy, and Callie and their family
Sarah, Emily, Melanie, Shane, Judy, and Frank—EM

Contents

Cool Cats

Mysterious, playful, skilled hunters, cuddly—cats are all of these things. From being revered as gods in ancient Egypt to being featured in Internet videos, felines fascinate us.

Cats can even change history. These animals have saved people's lives during wars. They've inspired inventors, musicians, and writers and exposed spies. Born with the instinct to hunt, cats are "hired" to control rodent populations in libraries, factories, and even museums! Some felines are so tuned in to how humans feel that they can predict when patients are about to pass away.

There's no "pussyfooting around" (which means to avoid the truth)—cats are the world's most popular pet. Researchers estimate there may be as many as 600 million pet cats in the world. The largest number of these live in the United States, where there are more than 75 million pet cats. No wonder something terrific is described as the "cat's meow," "cat's pajamas," or "cat's whiskers."

If it's "raining cats and dogs," people know to stay inside unless they want to look like "something the cat dragged in." The stage that models strut along is called a "catwalk," since they have to walk it as lightly as a cat does. Today, a "cool cat" means anyone who's savvy and hip. But originally, it was a top jazz musician who was skilled and as aloof as a cat.

Because cats have lived with people for at least 9,500 years, there are many legends and superstitions about them—especially about black ones. But it's no myth that owning a cat makes you healthier. According to a number of medical studies, petting a cat is calming and cat owners are less likely to have high blood pressure or heart disease. A cat can even learn to detect when its owner is sad and may meow and cuddle more to try to make her feel happier.

Many people think cats only hang out with humans to get fed, but scientists have shown that felines actually think people are—well, the cat's meow! A study carried out in 2017 by researchers at Oregon State University proved that cats love buddying up with people even more than they like food, toys, or even catnip.

Cats have flown into space, helped police with cases, and tracked down smugglers. The "cat's out of the bag" (which means the secret's been revealed)—cats are amazing animals!

Cat Gods

Cat Worship in Ancient Egypt

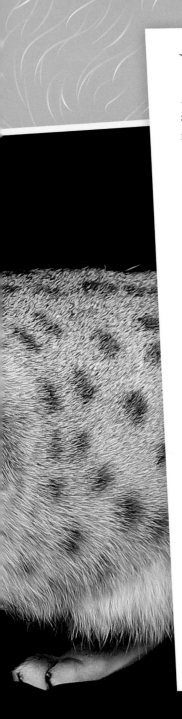

Miut stretched and yawned. She'd had her usual breakfast of the most delicious lamb, fish, pork, and eggs her owners could provide. It had been so good that she hadn't even helped herself to meat from her master's plate. Royal cats might be fed even better food, but Miut was very content with how her family treated her.

Sniffing the air, Miut decided to walk through her small village to see if anything interesting was happening. Yesterday, she and her master had ridden in his horse-drawn chariot near a river where they'd spent the day hunting. In the morning, Miut had raced through the grasses to retrieve birds her master had shot with his bow and arrow. Then, in the afternoon, she'd fetched fish for him from the edge of the water.

Just thinking about that fish made Miut hungry. So she headed to the marketplace. She passed a whole family of people—a father, mother, and their four children—with shaved eyebrows. But Miut hardly noticed anything odd about it, since she'd seen it so often.

As she loped past the stalls on her long, black-striped legs, the owners offered her tidbits of meat or chunks of fish to show how much they honored and respected cats. She gobbled them down, licked her whiskers, and kept going.

The Egyptian sun beat down on the village, so Miut slipped inside a storehouse full of grain to rest for a moment. But she soon realized she wasn't alone. Her pale green eyes widened as she peered about. As she crept through the dusty gloom, her gray-beige fur with its dark spots camouflaged her.

Then suddenly, she saw it—a snake! Miut silently edged closer and lowered herself into an attack crouch. With one pounce, she was on the wriggling beast. A quick bite just behind the snake's head, and soon the hunter was crunching down on her lunch.

Ancient Egyptians believed that if they wore amulets (charms) of cats, cat goddess Bastet would protect them.

Meow!

The people of ancient Mesopotamia (today's Iraq and surrounding area) likely domesticated cats as early as 8000 BCE, long before the Egyptians did.

Miut started to think about the cozy bed waiting for her in her house. As she headed back, she passed a house on fire. Most of the people rushed about frantically with water, but there was a line of men standing outside the blazing building. The men became very worried when they noticed Miut and carefully watched her until she was safely past the fiery site.

The sun was sinking when Miut ambled into her home. The children rushed to pat her and play with her. After supper, while the family relaxed together, Miut crawled under her mistress's chair, curled herself up, and was soon fast asleep, happily dreaming of mice and birds.

Pest Control

In ancient Egypt, the most honored and revered animal was the cat. The relationship between Egyptians and felines began around 2000 BCE when farmers were trying to solve the problem of mice and rats eating their grain and other food. Someone noticed African wildcats hunting the pests and began to leave out treats, such as fish heads, to encourage the cats to visit regularly.

The cats appreciated the easy food supply of both prey and snacks. Living close to humans kept them safe from larger predators too. Soon, cats were welcomed into the Egyptians' houses. The felines hunted the poisonous snakes, stinging scorpions, and dirty rodents that crept into the homes. The humans provided the cats with a safe place to raise their kittens.

It's a Crime to Kill a Cat

In their homes, the cats ate the finest wild birds, goat meat, and even honey cakes and were allowed to help themselves to anything on the master's plate. Despite their love of cats, Egyptians rarely gave their pets names.

Female cats—tame or wild—were mostly called Miut ("she who mews") while males were named Miu ("he who mews").

When a cat died, a priest inspected the corpse to make sure it had died naturally. It was a crime to kill a cat, even accidentally, and the penalty was death.

Then the cat's owners began weeks of mourning. This included everyone in the household shaving their eyebrows to show their sorrow. (The mourning period was over when people's eyebrows had grown back.) They also held elaborate funerals where they beat their chests to express their grief.

Ancient Egyptians were very concerned about keeping cats safe and healthy. If a house caught fire, a line of men surrounded the flaming building. Their sole job was to watch out for nearby cats that might be attracted by the heat of the blaze and keep them out of danger.

Around 1500 BCE people began to create tomb paintings showing cats as part of everyday life.

Bastet, Mafdet, and Neith

It wasn't long after the Egyptians domesticated cats that people began to closely connect them with many gods and goddesses. The most famous cat goddess was Bastet, a symbol for family and home. A huge cult developed around her. Early statues, paintings, and stone carvings of Bastet showed her with a lion's head because it was thought she was fierce like a lion.

Bastet's image gradually became gentler and she was associated more with pet cats. Because of this connection, ancient Egyptians placed statues of cats outside their houses to protect their families and keep evil spirits away.

The goddess of justice, Mafdet, also had the head of a lion and was believed to protect people against snakes and scorpions. Neith was a goddess of war who sometimes took the form of a cat.

Bastet had a cat's head and the body of a woman. Her name means "devouring lady."

Cyrus Surprise

When archaeologists discovered an ordinary-looking grave on the island of Cyprus in the Mediterranean Sea in 1983, they found something that shocked them.

The grave site dated back to 7500 BCE and contained a human skeleton, along with stone tools and seashells. But just inches away was the skeleton of a kitten. It had been carefully placed facing the same direction as the human. That told the archaeologists that the little cat was probably a pet, meaning that people had been keeping felines as pets about for 6,000 years longer than scientists had previously known.

Cat-astrophe

In 525 BCE, the Persian army invaded Egypt. But no matter how hard the Persians pushed forward, the Egyptians stopped them at the important trading city of Pelusium.

Then the Persian general Cambyses II had an idea. He had his soldiers paint images of the goddess Bastet on their shields. As the men surged into battle, they also released cats onto the battlefield, as well as dogs and sheep and other animals the Egyptians honored. Some reports said the Persians were even holding cats in their arms.

This wily trick meant the Egyptians were helpless to defend themselves—they knew that if they killed a cat even by accident, the penalty would be death. Their general surrendered the city rather than harm the cats. Cambyses was crowned pharaoh of Egypt and the Persians ruled the country for more than 100 years.

The cat cult was a religious movement in Egypt from about 1600 BCE until 390 CE. That's when the cult was banned as Christianity became an important religion in the country.

This painting from an Egyptian temple shows the goddess Mafdet.

Cats were usually mummified with their arms and legs close to their bodies, like this mummy, or in a sitting position.

From the Cat-acombs

Most people know that ancient Egyptians made people into mummies when they died. But as long ago as 1000 BCE, cats were also mummified and buried in their own underground tombs, called catacombs, in Egypt. (The word *catacomb* doesn't actually have anything to do with cats, but it may be based on a Latin phrase that means "among the tombs.")

To make the cat mummies, the cloth was wrapped in intricate patterns. Some mummies had faces painted on in gold or black, with glass or crystal eyes. The mummies were sometimes placed in small sarcophagi (coffins).

In 1888, an Egyptian farmer discovered a mass grave of thousands of cat mummies. Some of the mummies can now be seen in London's British Museum. But there were so many of them that they were considered almost worthless and most were ground up and sold as fertilizer!

Smugglers Beware!

Cats were so valuable to the Egyptians that smuggling a cat out of the country was punishable by death. Military records show soldiers being sent off to retrieve missing cats. But a group of people known as the Phoenicians were likely the first to catnap felines out of Egypt. These people lived around the east end of the Mediterranean Sea and were well known as sailors and traders.

The Phoenicians sold the stolen cats to wealthy people in Athens, Greece, and other large cities to hunt mice and rats. By 1000 BCE, cats had spread throughout the Mediterranean area. Even today, all around the world, many farmers, factory owners, and even museums (see page 62) depend on cats to keep pests under control.

Egyptians took cats hunting with them to retrieve game, especially from marshes.

Spotted Speedster

The cats you see in ancient Egyptian art are Egyptian maus, probably the oldest breed of cat in the world. Mau is the Egyptian word for "cat." They're one of the few naturally spotted breeds of domestic cats, with black dots on their light gray coats. This breed is also known for its big green eyes.

Many Egyptian Maus have an "M" marking on their foreheads. Their eyes may change from green to turquoise.

With its hind legs longer than its front legs, the Egyptian mau is an excellent jumper and fast runner—these cats have been clocked at 50 kilometers (30 miles) per hour!

Brighter Fur, Shrinking Brain

Living with people changed cats. Over thousands of years, their fur evolved to became more colorful, since they no longer had to be so camouflaged for hunting. Their bodies became smaller and less well muscled as their diets changed from rodents or snakes to cooked food. Cats' activities also shifted from hunting to lounging.

Survival instincts became less important, so their brains shrunk. The size of their adrenal and pituitary glands also decreased. These organs are responsible for an animal's "fight or flight" response and cats' safety and survival no longer depended on this. Cats also obviously even learned to put up with people!

The First Cats

Cats in ancient Egypt were some of the world's first pet cats. But their earliest ancestor appeared long before that. *Proailurus*—its name means "first cat"—lived about 34 million years ago. It was slightly larger than a pet cat today, with a tail almost as long as its body, large eyes, and sharp teeth and claws.

About 23 million years ago, cats' best-known ancestor first appeared. Saber-toothed cats had eye teeth, or canines, that never stopped growing and could be as long as 15 centimeters (6 inches). The most famous saber tooth was *Smilodon*—its name is Greek for "carving knife tooth."

Smilodon is one of the most famous prehistoric mammals ever.

Pseudaelurus was North America's first feline. This cat was the size of a modern cougar and lived about 20 million years ago. It hunted prey in Africa, Asia, and Europe and crossed the land bridge from Siberia to what's now Alaska.

Between 11 and 6 million years ago, the ancestors of lions, tigers, servals, and other wild cats appeared. These cats lived in Africa, Asia, Europe, and South America.It took almost 3 million more years for the ancestors of pet cats to show up in Africa.

The cats that ancient Egyptians tamed were African wildcats. They became distinct from their ancestors about 20,000 years ago. Today's pet cats evolved from these felines about 8,000 years ago. The scientific name for the domestic or house cat is *Felis silvestris catus—felis* is the Latin word for "cat." This is where the word *feline* comes from.

Most modern cats are descended from the cats of ancient Egyptians. Cats often seem to act as if they think they should still be treated with as much honor as their ancestors were!

The serval is a long-legged wild cat that lives in Africa.

Bad Luck Cats

Black Cats and the Black Death in Medieval Europe

The jet-black cat stood meowing just inside the door of the tumbledown cottage.

"Dost thou wish to go out, Gyb?" asked his owner, Siusan, coming to the door. "Couldst thee wait until later? It will be darker then and no one will see thee.

"Ever since that pope declared you cats evil, I worry whenever you go out," Siusan continued. "That was not so many years ago and people remember it well. It's not your fault, but people can be very nasty to black cats like you."

Looking pointedly at the door, Gyb just meowed.

"So be it." Siusan sighed, opening the door. "Out thou goest. But be careful. Don't stay out all night—come back before the morrow."

Trotting down a lane, Gyb's golden eyes gleamed in the darkness. Usually, he headed out with his brother Brinley, a tabby. But Brinley was curled up at home sniffing and sneezing today. Gyb never seemed to get sick, even though he licked and groomed his brother.

As he walked along, Gyb stopped to take a quick lick or two at his coat. He'd spent a lot of time in the bright sunshine this summer, and his coat had turned much lighter. But now, in late September, it was almost completely inky black again.

Suddenly, two men came rushing along the lane. Gyb slunk under the bushes just in time and crouched there motionless.

"I tell thee, I saw a cat and a black one, too. It could be the devil," yelled one of the men.

In the cool dimness, Gyb watched them warily. Luckily, he blended into the shadows and was nearly invisible.

This painting of a black cat and its prey dates back to about 1236.

When Humans Were Kibble

Scientists who study human evolution think the reason some people believe black cats are bad luck may date back to prehistoric times. Back then, many cats were much, much larger than they are now and they liked to snack on our ancestors. No wonder people were afraid of cats. As cats became smaller, some people overcame their fear of felines, but not everyone did.

Add to that the fact that in the Middle Ages, some people believed ravens were a sign that death was near. Ravens are black, so it wasn't long before some people began to associate cats—an animal many already distrusted—that were black with death and bad luck.

"Well, if it be a cat, let's leave the poor beast alone," said the other man. "And if it be the devil, let's hope he leaves us alone. Come along now, let's go home."

Gyb stayed in the bushes until he was sure the men were gone. A mouse scampering by didn't notice him. Gyb considered giving chase and catching a snack, but remembered Siusan would have dinner waiting for him at home.

The thought of his food dish suddenly made Gyb hungry. With a lick of his black paw pads and a twitch of his tail, he stretched out his front legs and began ambling homeward. After all, he couldn't take a chance that Brinley might get more food than he did!

In 1579 a pamphlet against witchcraft was published in England. It included this drawing and told how some women keep spirits that look like cats.

Devil Cats

In medieval times (approximately 500 CE to 1300 CE), people were suspicious of cats—not only black ones but those of any color. In 1232, Pope Gregory IX of the Catholic Church issued a document stating they were "diabolical." At that time, Europe was mostly Catholic, which meant that, thanks to Pope Gregory, almost everyone in Europe began to fear and hate cats.

The pope claimed that cats were used in devil worship rituals and likened the devil to a cat. People of the time thought evil spirits came out at night, when cats also liked to roam. They believed felines were bad because they aren't mentioned in the Bible.

This early 1400s' painting shows a black cat peeking out from hell.

In October 1555, these three women were accused of being witches and burned in northern Germany.

Burn the Witch!

Because cats were associated with the devil, and so also with witchcraft, owning a cat could result in a person being sentenced to death. Tens of thousands of people, mostly women, were killed for being witches from the 1300s to the 1700s. In Europe, they were burned at the stake. In North America, they were hanged. Many of them were elderly widows or unmarried women who lived alone or had no one looking out for them.

Millions of cats associated with these so-called witches were slaughtered with their owners. Europe's cat population—especially black cats—was almost wiped out. Even today, the percentage of black cats in Europe is lower than in most other parts of the world.

The Black Death Strikes

Unfortunately, for people in Europe, the killing of cats happened at the same time as the spread of the Black Death in the mid-1300s. This deadly disease was likely caused by bubonic plague, which spread from Central Asia. It was carried throughout Europe by fleas living on the rats that often hitched rides on ships.

The Black Death caused swollen lumps (called buboes, which give the bubonic plague its name) in the armpit, groin, and neck. Black spots appeared on the victim's skin, followed by high fever and vomiting blood. People rarely recovered from it.

By the 1400s, there were few cats left to chase mice away from homes. So like the man shown here, people had to do it themselves.

The Staring Cat

Perhaps one reason people in medieval times were scared of cats is because they were unnerved by the way felines seem to stare at nothing. They actually may be looking at things the human eye can't see.

Cats' eyes are great at detecting motion. They see sunlight on specks of dust and microscopic insects. Since felines also hear better than humans, they sense things like a floorboard creaking and will turn toward it. The cat may be listening, not staring.

With its sensitive nose, a cat can notice faint smells and pivot for a better sniff. Its whiskers pick up vibrations, so the feline will turn toward even small movements like a slight breeze.

The Cat Came Back

While the Black Death was spreading from town to town, some regions made it illegal to own a cat. Despite this, a few people kept their pets. Eventually, other people noticed that the cat owners often seemed to be safe from the sickness. More and more townsfolk observed this, and in the 1500s, the word began to spread.

Once people realized that rats were responsible for spreading the plague, everyone wanted to own a cat or two. Soon, laws were made to protect cats, since people now realized how valuable they were to public health.

The Oriental rat flea spread the Black Death by drinking a diseased rat's blood, then biting a human.

Rats Gone Wild

It wasn't long before people blamed cats—not just the black ones, but all of them—for the Black Death. But the opposite was true. The rat population in Europe soared without cats around, so the disease-carrying fleas had lots of furry homes.

Over about 300 years, the Black Death killed as many as 50 million people in Europe, or more than half the population. Because of the number of people who died, European society and its economy were shattered. With improved hygiene and quarantines, the epidemic was finally brought under control in the 1700s. It's likely the Black Death wouldn't have taken nearly so many lives if people hadn't allowed the rat population to explode by killing most of Europe's cats.

Lucky or Unlucky?

In modern times, in North America, black cats are still considered bad luck. The Pilgrims who came to America from England in 1620 may be responsible for that. They were very religious and therefore suspicious of black cats, whom they thought were part demon.

But black cats are now considered good luck in Australia, Great Britain, and Japan. Fishermen's wives in England used to keep black cats at home to protect their husbands at sea. In Scotland, some people believe a cat visiting a home brings wealth. In Holland, there are people who think you shouldn't tell secrets in front of a cat because it will tell your neighbors.

In Japan, there's a superstition that a woman who owns a black cat will have many boyfriends. In Germany, if a black cat crosses a person's path from left to right, that's good luck. But if the cat walks from right to left, watch out!

There are also lots of superstitions around cats and weather. When a cat washes its ears, rain is coming. A cat sleeping with all four paws tucked under means bad weather is on the way. Sailors believed that if cats were upset, they could start storms through magic in their tails. So ships' cats were always kept well fed and happy!

Meow!

In the same way people's hair turns gray or white as they age, so does cat fur. On black cats, it's very noticeable.

In Japan and Britain a black cat crossing your path is supposed to bring good luck. But in North America and some European countries, it's bad luck.

Most black cats have gold eyes, but some have green or orange eyes. Like all cats, their eyes are blue when they're born.

Meow!

On Black Friday (the day following American Thanksgiving), many animal shelters in North America encourage the adoption of black cats.

The Secrets in the Genes

Ebony cats are known to be good hunters, perhaps because their dark coats help them blend into the shadows. The dark fur is due to high levels of the pigment melanin (a pigment is a substance that causes color). Melanin also makes most black cats have gold-colored eyes.

Black cats seem to be healthier and have better immune systems than other cats. The same gene that makes the fur black is similar to genes that make some people resistant to diseases such as human immunodeficiency virus (HIV). (Genes are the part of a cell that decides what characteristics are passed from a parent to a child.) Someday, black cats may prove to be very lucky for people, if researchers can unlock the secret linking their genetic material, strong immunity, and inky color. How would Pope Gregory feel to discover that the black cats he hated so much may one day save people from diseases?

Eyes and Nose of a Hunter

Black cats are especially good hunters, but all cats have keen senses to help them catch prey. Most importantly, cats have excellent night vision. They can see at just one-sixth of the light that humans need. Humans have round pupils (the black part in the middle of the eye) but cats have vertical-slit pupils. This shape helps them see better at night and estimate where to jump when they ambush prey.

Humans can hear sounds with frequencies up to 20,000 hertz (a unit for measuring sound), while cats can hear up to 100,000 hertz, which allows them to hear mice and other prey squeaking. Cats can swivel their ears to pinpoint subtle sounds. Each cat ear has 32 muscles that allow it to rotate. People have only six muscles in each ear.

The ear movement helps cats locate sound with extreme accuracy. As well, the furry tufts on the inside of a cat's ears direct sound into their ears, help keep out dirt, and insulate the ears. This fluff is called "ear furnishings."

Cats have 200 million scent receptors—you only have 5 million. Cats can sniff out where you've been and who's been hanging out with you. But because their noses are so sensitive, cats dislike strong smells and may even find them painful.

A cat has other senses that allow it to find its way home, even over great distances. Scientists don't know how they do it, but felines can also predict storms and earthquakes with great accuracy. A few hours or even a few days before an earthquake, some cats act frightened and anxious. They may meow a lot, run away, or look for places to hide.

Good Luck Cats

The Cat That Saved the Samurai

Many, many years ago in Japan, there lived a poor temple priest near Tokyo. The temple was old and broken-down, just like the holy man. Although the priest had barely enough food for himself, he took in a cat, which he called Tama.

Despite his thinness, the stray was a handsome cat. He was mostly white with black and orange patches and a very short tail.

Few people came to the temple with gifts of money or food. Soon, the priest and Tama were nearly starving.

One day, Tama was sitting in front of the temple as a thunderstorm crackled overhead. Unconcerned, he groomed himself. He licked his left front paw, then used it to clean his left ear, as cats are careful to do.

Tama was about to clean his right ear when the storm broke. Torrents of rain poured down on the ramshackle temple. Luckily, the cat was dry under the overhang of the building's roof.

But Tama noticed a lordly samurai warrior and his men galloping through the driving rain. As the cat watched, the group stopped to shelter under a tree.

Soon Tama went back to his washing. He licked his right paw and turned his attention to scrubbing his right ear.

The samurai noticed the cat. In Japan, when people beckon to each other, they turn the palm of their hand toward the person they want to come closer. So to the samurai, the grooming cat looked as if he were inviting the nobleman to come closer.

A beckoning cat! How extraordinary, the astonished samurai must have thought. This was obviously a summons not to be ignored. So the men took up the reins of their horses and hurried toward the temple.

The priest at the ramshackle old temple said his prayers using a loop of prayer beads.

Meow!

Maneki-neko is also known as the fortune cat, happy cat, lucky cat, money cat, and welcoming cat.

A maneki-neko usually has a decoration around its neck. This is sometimes a scarf but a collar and bell are more common.

Suddenly—CRACK! Lightning hit the tree where the men had taken refuge, and down fell an enormous branch. The cat had saved the men's lives. The samurai and his followers entered the temple, where they were welcomed by the priest. Tama simply continued grooming himself.

The samurai was so grateful to Tama and the priest that the warrior rebuilt the temple and showered it with riches. The priest and Tama had plenty to eat from then on.

And so the legend of the lucky beckoning cat, or maneki-neko (ma-NECK-ee-NECK-o) was passed down through the ages.

Samurai were nobles trained in military tactics and strategy. Their culture still affects Japanese culture.

Lots of Lucky Cats

The story of Tama is just one of the tales told about the origin of the maneki-neko. One tells of a poor shopkeeper who fed a stray cat. To thank him, the cat beckoned customers into the store, which then became so popular that the shopkeeper became rich. Another story tells of a cat that waved at a nobleman who was traveling along a path. The man walked off the trail toward the cat. That was when he realized the cat had saved him from walking into a trap set by thieves just ahead on the path.

There's also a tale about how a waving cat saved his mistress from a poisonous snake, and a story about an ancient Japanese emperor who was brought good luck by a cat beckoning to a wealthy businessman. Another tale describes how a poor woman had to sell her cat because she could no long afford to feed it. In a dream, he told her to make statues of him with his paw up. She sold them and became rich.

According to legend, a beckoning cat also helped an emperor called Huwormishu, who lived almost 1,500 years ago. In the legend, the emperor was allergic to cats and banned them from his palace. But his son Prince Togamashu fell in love with a stray cat, brought it home, and hid it. When Huwormishu found the cat, he banished his son and the cat from the palace.

One day, a wealthy businessman was on his way to the palace to meet with the emperor. When the man passed by Togamashu's new home, the prince's cat waved at him. The businessman was amazed. When he arrived at the palace, he told Huwormishu that he had planned to refuse to make a business deal with him. But he had changed his mind when he saw the beckoning cat. The emperor was so relieved that the cat had made the businessman rethink his decision that he welcomed Togamashu and his lucky cat back into the palace.

Dick Whittington and His Cat

Dick Whittington was a poor servant boy living in England in the 1300s. His master told Dick and his other servants to find something to send on his ship heading to the Barbary Coast (North Africa) that could be sold to make money. All Dick could send was his cat.

The court of the king of Barbary was overrun with mice, so Dick's cat became incredibly valuable and the ship returned to England full of riches for Dick. He later became mayor of London.

Dick Whittington did become mayor of London in 1397, but he likely never had a cat. No one knows how the story of Dick's cat, said to have brought him luck, started.

Puss in Boots

Did you know that Puss in Boots from the *Shrek* movies is based on a fairy tale? Like the story of the maneki-neko, it's about a cat that brings its owner luck.

In this tale, a son inherits a cat when his father dies. The cat promises to make the young man rich if he'll buy the cat boots. Puss in Boots then catches a rabbit, which he presents to the king from his master.

The cat also outsmarts an ogre and takes over his castle. The boy marries the king's daughter and Puss in Boots lives as a great lord. The story is world famous and in French is known as *Le Chat botté* (as seen in this illustration).

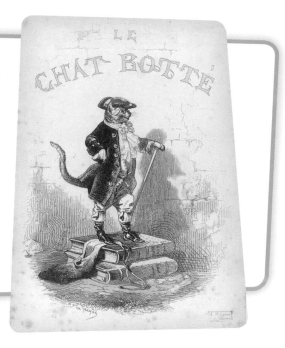

The Pointing Paw

Today, you'll see ceramic or plastic figurines of the beckoning cat in many Japanese stores and restaurants. Although this lucky charm originated in Japan during the 1900s, it quickly spread to China. The maneki-neko is used in feng shui (fung SHWAY), a Chinese philosophy for arranging furniture and buildings for luck and harmony. Beckoning cats can also be seen in many Chinese stores and restaurants. Chinese immigrants helped the maneki-neko spread around the world.

Today, most maneki-neko are made of ceramic or plastic. They can be figurines, piggy banks, and even key chains.

The most common color for a maneki-neko is white, said to bring happiness and positive energy. Gold figurines are believed to bring money, and black ones repel evil.

If the right paw of the maneki-neko is raised, the cat will bring good luck. When the left paw is up, more customers will come. If the maneki-neko has both paws raised, the cat is inviting in both money and customers. The higher the maneki-neko's paw, the more money or customers will come, or they'll come from a greater distance.

This cat wants to be friends. You can tell by its upright tail with a curl at the end.

Meow, Meow, Meow

The maneki-neko communicates with its paws, but cats have many ways to communicate. If a cat presses and pushes at you with her paws as if she's giving you a massage, she's saying you're officially her territory.

Cats often meow at people but rarely at other cats. Some researchers think this is because they can use body language with one another, but people haven't yet learned to understand it. Other scientists say that cats are trying to imitate human speech or that they have learned that meowing at people will get them what they want!

When a cat purrs or growls, you can probably easily guess what she is trying to tell you. But did you know that if she chirps, she's saying she's excited? And if she makes loud, rapid, repeated sounds, she's telling you she's anxious?

Cats don't just communicate with their voices. If a cat's ears are up and facing forward, it means she's interested in what's going on. But look out if her ears are back and flat on her head—she's angry. When one ear is up and the other is flat, it shows the cat's not sure what to do.

A cat's tail can talk too. If its tail is straight up with a curl at the end, the cat is feeling friendly. But if its tail is straight up with the fur fluffed out, the cat senses a threat.

If you want to tell your cat that you love her, crouch down and slowly blink at her. That says, "I'm happy." If she blinks back, blink again to keep the conversation going.

The Prime Minister's Good Luck Cat

During World War II, a ship's cat named Blackie was lucky for Britain's prime minister Winston Churchill and for the world. Churchill arrived in Newfoundland in August 1941 aboard the HMS *Prince of Wales* for a secret meeting with American president Franklin D. Roosevelt.

As Churchill was leaving the ship, Blackie scampered forward and Churchill, a cat lover, stopped to pat him. Later Churchill thought the little cat must have brought him luck because he got the agreement that he wanted from the Americans about how they and other countries battling on their side would work together with the British to fight the Nazis. Blackie was renamed Churchill and went on to be even luckier—he survived the sinking of his ship later that year.

British prime minister Winston Churchill patting Blackie. At home, Churchill wouldn't eat dinner without his cat Jock nearby.

The Real Maneki-neko

Maneki-neko are based on a breed called the Japanese bobtail. This cat is known for its short, or bobbed, tail. The little curved tail has a pom-pom of longer fur at its end. (The most famous tailless cats are Manx cats, which originated on the Isle of Man, off Britain's coast.)

The most popular fur color pattern for Japanese bobtails is black, orange, and white, known as tricolor or calico (shown here). Tama, the first beckoning cat, was said to be a calico, so this combination is considered the luckiest maneki-neko.

The Luck of McHamish

A cat named Hamish McHamish brought fame and luck to the town of St. Andrews, Scotland. Although he had a home and an owner, in the early 2000s, this handsome, long-haired ginger cat spent his days around various businesses, attracting tourists. Hamish was lucky for the town because people visited especially so they could have photos taken with him. While in St. Andrews, the tourists spent money in the town's shops and cafés, so the store and restaurant owners thought Hamish brought them lots of good fortune.

Hamish had a Facebook page and the local bookstore set up a "Hamish recommends" section—the books in it were fish cookbooks and stories about cats. Although Hamish died in 2014, a statue in the town reminds people of this famous lucky cat.

Hamish even had a book written about him.

Paw Prints in History

Although the story of the maneki-neko was likely first told sometime in the 1600s or 1700s, the beckoning statue was first written about in a history of Japan published in 1852. Hundreds of years before this, famous Japanese artists made paintings of cats. There are many Japanese folktales about cats. The cats in these stories aren't always lucky, like the maneki-neko, but they are often smart and sly.

One of the most famous books in the country's classic literature is *I Am a Cat*, by Soseki Natsume. This novel for adults was written more than 100 years ago. In it, a snobby cat observes the lives of Japanese people he knows and makes witty comments about them.

Adoring crowds take pictures of cats sleeping on a blossoming cherry tree in Tokyo.

Cats on Track

Cats don't just bring good luck to humans. They also help racehorses run faster by keeping them calm. Gator Kitten at Toronto's Woodbine Racetrack often sits with a horse named Tap the Pistol, which soothes the racer. Gator Kitten has a Twitter account where you can see photos of the racetrack.

Racehorses spend as much as 21 hours daily in a stall, so cats provide variety in their day, as well as keeping mice away. American horse Indiana Charlie loves calico cat Mugsy. The feline visits the horse many times a day and Indiana Charlie loves to lick and groom the little cat—see their video online.

Cat Islands and Cat Town

Cats are still incredibly beloved in Japan, partly because they're believed to be lucky. Another reason is that they're little, so they fit into Japanese homes, which tend to be small.

Off the coast of Japan are more than ten "cat islands," popular tourist sites where the felines far outnumber the humans. About 100 years ago, silkworms were raised on the island of Tashirojima. Cats chased the mice away from the valuable worms, and the feline population grew until there are now about six times as many cats as people here and on other islands.

In northern Japan, a cat named Tama became stationmaster at a railway station in 2007. Ridership surged because she was a major tourist attraction with her special hat and two cat assistants.

The city of Tokyo is full of cat sites. The Yanaka neighborhood is called Cat Town because cats wander all over the area. People in Tokyo also eat steamed buns, cakes, and pizzas decorated to look like cats, or visit a bookstore that only sells cat-themed books.

People believe the temple where the original Tama invited the samurai to take shelter is Tokyo's Gotokuji Temple. Shelves there are crammed with hundreds of maneki-neko that people have left to bring them luck.

Japanese people love cats, in towns (left) or on one of the cat islands (right).

Meow!

In Italy, hearing a cat sneeze is good luck. Some people in Japan believe a grooming cat (of any color) means company is coming.

Inspiring Cats

Electric Cat

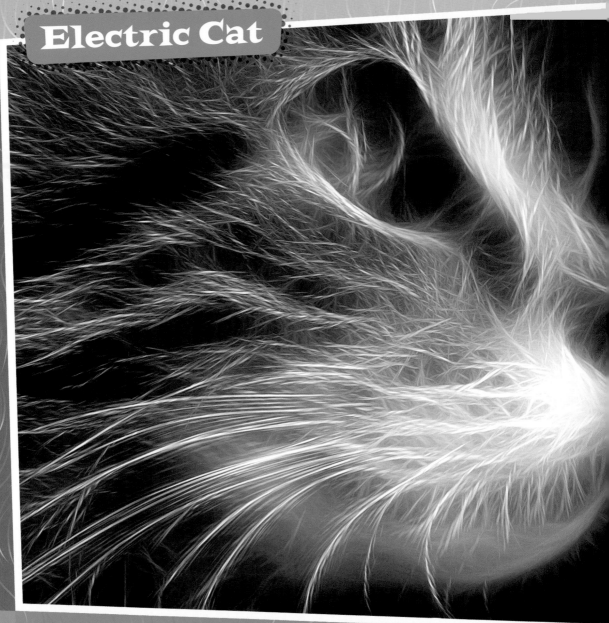

Little Nikola Tesla loved his cat Mačak (which means "male cat" in Serbian). The two of them happily played together in the small village of Smiljan (in today's Croatia, in central Europe), where Nikola was born in 1856.

Nikola said Mačak was the finest of all cats in the world and the pet followed him everywhere. If Mačak felt Nikola was in danger from another person or animal, the cat would fluff out his fur to twice his normal size, arch his back, and stick his tail straight up in the air. The angry cat would howl his rage until he felt Nikola was safe again. The boy called his pet "The Magnificent Mačak."

These two best friends ran through the village or rolled on the grass together, the big cat purring with happiness. But Mačak hated getting his paws wet, so on rainy days, they'd find a warm, cozy place to play indoors.

When Nikola was three years old, his village was caught in the grip of a freezing cold snap. The town was high in the mountains. Air becomes drier the higher it is above sea level, so the air in his town was incredibly dry. There was so little moisture in the mountain air that when people walked in the snow, they left a trail of glowing footprints behind them. When children threw snowballs, the packed snow exploded with a bright flare of light when it hit anything.

Around dusk one night in that cold, dry winter, Nikola was patting his beloved cat. The little boy was amazed—with every stroke, his hand produced a shower of sparks. The crackling sounds that accompanied the light were loud enough to be heard across the room. Mačak's back was a sheet of light.

As the night grew darker, Nikola's parents lit candles to light their home. Mačak had begun to walk away when Nikola noticed his favorite playmate was shaking his paws as though he was walking on something irritating or wet. When Nikola looked more closely, he saw that Mačak was surrounded by a dim halo of light.

> Mačak was a large cat like this one and was Nikola's closest friend. This pet inspired his master to change how the world is powered.

Furr-ensic Data

Cats also inspire detectives. A woman named Shirley Duguay disappeared in Prince Edward Island, Canada, in October 1994. Police suspected her husband, Douglas Beamish, of murdering her. But they had no evidence.

The police discovered a jacket with Duguay's blood on it. As well, they found pale cat hairs on the coat's lining—could they have come from Beamish's white cat, Snowball?

Human DNA (deoxyribonucleic acid) evidence has long been used to solve crimes, but no one had ever convicted a murderer using genetic material from an animal. Scientists proved the fur belonged to Snowball and convicted Beamish. Since then, several cases in North America have been solved using animal DNA.

Meow!

Famous nurse Florence Nightingale felt cats had "more sympathy and feeling than human beings." You can still see the paw prints her cats left on her letters.

The fantastic sights of that night stayed with Nikola. He began a lifelong quest to understand electricity. Nikola later wrote, "I cannot exaggerate the effect of this marvelous night on my childish imagination. Day after day I have asked myself, 'What is electricity?'"

Thanks to Mačak, Nikola Tesla became an inventor, an engineer, and an innovator far ahead of his time. Some people say that Nikola Tesla and his inventions and discoveries changed the world. His work was inspired by his cat, Mačak.

Electricity can make you see sparks when you bite a hard candy or rip a piece of tape off the roll in the dark. It can also make your hair stand on end!

Tesla in America

When Tesla was in his mid-twenties, he began working in Paris, France, for the Continental Edison Company, a company founded by the famous inventor Thomas Alva Edison. Two years later, Tesla moved to the United States to work for Edison's company in New York City.

It was there that Tesla became best known for helping to design the alternating current (AC) electrical supply system, which powers the world today. It's the form of electrical energy people use when they plug in televisions, toasters, or lamps. Tesla also developed an AC power plant that harnessed the hydroelectric power of Niagara Falls.

His Tesla Coil magnifying transmitter could generate huge amounts of power—as well as a lightning bolt 40 meters (130 feet) long. Tesla also worked on wireless lighting and wireless communication. He created a remote-controlled boat and even worked on a machine to communicate with space aliens!

In 1899, in his lab in Colorado Springs, Colorado, Tesla set up his "magnifying transmitter," which generated millions of volts of electricity. The transmitter allowed for the wireless transmission of electrical energy.

Flying Sparks!

Why did Mačak fur glow and spark when young Nikola Tesla patted him? If you've ever shuffled over a carpet when you're wearing socks and felt sparks fly, then you've experienced the same phenomenon.

When the air is dry, a cat's fur becomes charged with static electricity—the same electricity that you felt. As a cat licks itself, the moisture in its saliva makes it easier for the electricity to "leak" off the cat's fur. When you pat the cat, you get zapped by this static electricity. Mačak felt this with every step he took, which is why he shook his paws.

Zzzzzap! You and your cat will both feel an electric shock if you stroke the cat's fur after shuffling across a wool carpet when you're wearing socks.

Meow!

Famous Spanish painter Pablo Picasso was inspired to include a black kitten in his painting, *Dora Maar au Chat (Dora Maar with Cat)*. It's now one of the world's most expensive paintings!

Electrifying Innovations

The sight of his cat, Mačak, glowing in the dark inspired Nikola Tesla. He studied electricity and learned to harness it. Thanks to Mačak, Tesla invented technological advancements that were far ahead of his time.

The Tesla is one of the world's top-selling plug-in electric cars. It's named after Nikola Tesla.

Tesla's work with electricity led to the development of antennas, fluorescent lights, MRI (Magnetic Resonance Imaging) scans, radar, radio, and tuners. The revolutionary electric car, the Tesla, is named after him. It's clear Tesla — and his cat!—still inspire science and our daily lives.

Cat's Eyes and Cheetah's Feet

Cats have influenced many inventors. In 1934, British inventor Percy Shaw created reflective road studs, known as "cats' eyes," after noticing how cats' eyes reflect light in the dark. Toshi Fukaya, a Japanese inventor, thought about how cats can retract their claws. He then invented a thumbtack with a point that stays covered until it's pushed into a wall.

American inventor Van Phillips was unhappy with the prosthetic (artificial) leg he was given following an accident. He studied how the long, elastic ligaments of the cheetah—the world's fastest animal—help these big cats race after prey (see page 52 to find out how fast a cheetah can run). In 1984, Phillips based the new leg he built on his findings, and today, most Paralympic athletes with a leg disability use a variation of the cheetah foot.

In 2013, inventors in Lausanne, France, built the cheetah-cub robot with legs modeled on the legs of a pet cat. This light, compact robot—it's about the size of a cat—runs just the way a feline does and may eventually be used in search-and-rescue missions or for exploring rough terrain.

A cheetah's legs are built for speed and its tough foot pads help it run over hard ground.

Paralympic athletes wearing a cheetah foot have broken many records. The foot is made of layers of carbon fiber.

E = mCat Squared

Many famous scientists, including Albert Einstein, were cat owners. The world's most important scientist ever, Englishman Sir Isaac Newton (1642–1727), loved cats. But during his experiments, his cat Spithead (named after a famous British battle) kept interrupting him by wanting to go in and out the door. Newton created the cat flap to keep Spithead happy.

Skipping over the Keys

Cats have inspired not only scientists and inventors. In 1739, after his cat Pucinella walked over a harpsichord keyboard, Italian composer Domenico Scarlatti wrote *Cat Fugue*. (A fugue is a piece of music with several melodies played at the same time.)

In 1838, Polish-French composer Frédéric Chopin wrote *The Cat Waltz* after his cat Valdeck walked over the piano keys. When American composer Zez Confrey heard a cat walk on a piano in 1921, he wrote *Kitten on the Keys*. You can find many of these songs on the Internet.

Famous physicist Albert Einstein owned a cat named Tiger—who became sad when it rained!

Cat Composer

In 1997, composer Morris Moshe Cotel was at his piano in New York City hoping for inspiration. Suddenly, his cat, Ketzel ("little cat" in Yiddish) jumped up on the instrument. She skipped over the keys and Cotel was amazed by what he heard. "This piece has a beginning, a middle, and an end," he said. "How can this be? It's written by a cat."

Cotel wrote down the 21-second-long song and sent it under Ketzel's name to a contest for short compositions in Paris. *Piece for Piano, Four Paws* won special mention and Ketzel earned money for it!

Many cats, like the one shown here, like to "play" the piano—you can see videos of them on-line.

"As Mysterious as a Cat"

Many writers love cats and are inspired by them. British author Neil Gaiman has lots of cats and has written about them on his blog. A black cat plays an important role in his book *Coraline*. "Authors like cats because they are such quiet, lovable, wise creatures," said twentieth-century Canadian writer Robertson Davies, "and cats like authors for the same reasons."

Getting Around

Nikola Tesla loved running and playing with his cat Mačak, and many inventors have been inspired by the way cats move. Cats have a lot of incredible features to help them leap, run, and stalk prey.

Most animals move the right front leg with the left back leg, and the left front leg at the same time as the right back one. But cats move their right front and right back legs together, then their left front and left back legs. This helps them walk quickly and quietly.

When cats walk, their back paws step almost exactly in the tracks of their front paws. This helps these hunters minimize their tracks. It also allows cats to walk on narrow ledges. And they can squeeze through small spaces thanks to their flexible shoulder blades. Human shoulder blades are attached by bone but a cat's are attached only by muscle, which is more flexible.

Cats walk and run on their tiptoes. With less of the foot touching the ground, there's less friction, which helps cats run fast. These hunters are built for short bursts of speed. They can also stay motionless for a long time when hunting prey.

Thanks to powerful leg and back muscles, a cat can jump up to six times its height. And if it falls, it will almost always land on its feet. That's because cats have a reflex that lets them twist in midair. Their soft paw pads and flexible joints absorb the shock of landing.

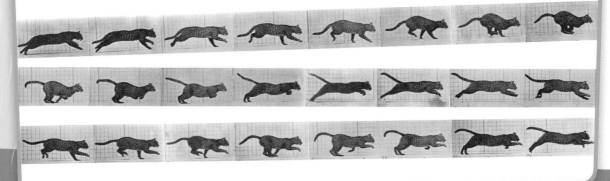

Canadian Lucy Maud Montgomery, the author of *Anne of Green Gables,* loved cats and often included them in her books. She even dedicated *Jane of Lantern Hill* to her cat Lucky.

American mystery and horror writer Edgar Allan Poe said, "I wish I could write as mysterious as a cat." His cat sat on his shoulder while he worked. Louisa May Alcott, who wrote the American children's classic *Little Women,* gave her characters cats and included a poem about one in her book. Edward Gorey, writer and artist of the macabre, loved cats and they inspired many of his illustrations. He once said, "Books. Cats. Life is good."

Many famous painters have also been inspired by cats. Artists such as Mary Cassatt, Leonardo da Vinci, Pablo Picasso, and Édouard Manet all included felines in their masterpieces.

In 1887, famous French painter Pierre-Auguste Renoir created this painting, *Julie Manet with Cat.* Julie was the daughter of friends of Renoir. By including a cat happily cradled on the little girl's lap, Renoir painted a calm, relaxed scene.

Feline Hunting

Tibbles the Exterminator

Machines

The sleek tabby slipped out the door and prowled through the low bushes. As he slunk around the rocks, the moon began to rise, lighting this hunter's path.

Since Tibbles the cat had come to Stephens Island, New Zealand, a few months ago, he'd gone out stalking prey almost every night. His owner, David Lyall, had brought Tibbles along when he became the assistant lighthouse keeper in 1894. Few people lived on this small, remote island off the south coast of New Zealand. Working at the lighthouse was a lonely job, so Lyall was glad to have Tibbles for company.

Tibbles had never seen anything like one of the little animals that lived on the island. It looked like a bird, but it never flew.

Instead, the tiny feathered creature scampered about like a mouse on its long legs. Its back was feathered in drab dark olive, and pale yellowish feathers covered its throat and chest. The bird was tiny like a mouse and had a stubby tail of short feathers.

By now, Tibbles knew its habits well. It made its nest in holes in the ground or under rocks and came out at night to eat small insects. That's why Tibbles was hunting by moonlight.

Catching one of these little things was difficult because they were so fast, but Tibbles had already hunted down a lot of them. He noticed that every night, it seemed he had to trek farther and farther from home before he tracked down any.

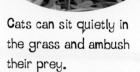

Cats can sit quietly in the grass and ambush their prey.

Cat Chatter

When an indoor cat spies a bird just outside the window, it crouches at the window, tail lashing back and forth, and sometimes it makes a strange chattering sound.

Scientists don't know why cats make this noise. Some think the feline is showing its frustration at not being able to get at its prey, while others think the cat is expressing its excitement at spotting the bird.

Some researchers believe that cats may be trying to imitate birdsong. The chattering also helps move air over the scent glands a cat has on the roof of its mouth, which allows it to learn more about its prey.

Meow!

A cat's paw pads are very sensitive, which gives the furry hunter lots of information about its prey, such as its location and texture and how lively it still is.

Tonight, Tibbles had loped quite a distance over the island's rough terrain before he found even one of the tiny birds. It was all alone, hopping about under the stars, snapping at insects and crunching them down with a gulp.

Tibbles watched for a few moments, his big eyes gleaming and his tail swishing back and forth. But the bird was totally unaware it was being observed by a deadly hunter. Tibbles tensed his muscles, gave a wriggle, and pounced . . .

Sometimes Tibbles ate his prey, but he had different plans for this bird. He grasped it tightly in his teeth, then trotted home through the brush and over the rocks.

The moon shone down its clear white light on Tibbles. The cat proudly dropped the bird on his master's doorstep and sat down to clean his whiskers.

Cats climb trees to get a better look at their surroundings.

Bird Nerd

Tibbles's owner, David Lyall, was a bird-watcher and he could identify many of the small fliers. But he'd never seen anything like the specimens that his cat kept leaving on his doorstep.

So Lyall sent one of the birds to a birding expert, who immediately realized it was a new species. Before cats had come to the island, there'd been no predators, so the wrens had lost the ability to fly. They'd become one of only a few flightless songbirds in the world. The birds had also likely lost any fear of possible predators since they had no experience with them.

A cat will often sway its head side to side just before it pounces. This helps it better judge exactly how far away the prey is so the hunter doesn't miss its target.

A New Species

The bird was named Stephens Island wren after the island where it was found. Some people also called it Lyall's wren in honor of the man who'd discovered it.

In early February 1895, searchers scoured the island looking for live specimens of the little bird but couldn't find a single Stephens Island wren. After a few more attempts to locate the birds, they gave up.

Within just a year of the Stephens Island wren being discovered, it was pronounced extinct. Because Tibbles had been known to prey on the birds, he was given all the blame for their total disappearance.

Hunting and Harming Habitats

Humans have contributed to the extinction of species in a number of ways. People have hunted many animals to extinction, from Australia's Tasmanian tiger to the passenger pigeon of the United States.

When people burn trees and grasses for development, clear-cut forests for wood, or bulldoze land to build on, they devastate animal habitats. If the animals can't successfully relocate, they often become extinct.

Another deadly situation can occur when people introduce new animals such as cats, dogs, and rats to an area. If the species already living there can't compete with the invasive animals for food or homes, they'll disappear forever.

Stephens Island wren once lived all over New Zealand, but by 1894, it could only be found on Stephens Island. It was also known as a rock wren because it ran quickly over rocks.

Community Cats

There were many feral cats on Stephens Island, and they likely helped drive the island's wren to extinction. Feral cats are stray cats. They have no owners and are too wild to ever be adopted.

In some cities in North America, these cats are known as community cats. They live in neighborhoods on their own or in colonies with other cats. Other community cats are strays: cats that once had homes but got lost. They can likely be adopted into new homes.

People often feed and care for cat colonies. These caregivers also try to neuter cats in a program known as Trap, Neuter, Return (TNR). (Neutering is an operation that prevents cats from having kittens.) This keeps the population of community cats from growing too quickly.

Born to Hunt

When Tibbles hunted the Stephens Island wren, he was just following his instincts. Cats are born with the urge to chase and hunt. Kittens as young as four weeks stalk and pounce on their food. Even if they're not taught how to hunt, kittens still become good hunters. Cats' vision is even designed to detect motion, including the movement of prey.

For cats, hunting is a survival instinct. Unlike most animals, feline bodies don't produce enough taurine, a substance animals need to make protein in order to build muscles, organs, and skin. Only meat provides enough taurine to keep a cat healthy.

Cats don't play with their prey before they kill it just for fun. A mouse or bird is fast and desperate when caught, and can hurt the cat badly with a sharp nip. Cats have short muzzles, so they need their prey to be almost motionless when they give it the fatal bite. The feline hunter tries to tire out its prey to make sure it can't escape or bite back.

Many felines that are provided with food still spend hours stalking prey. They may only kill their targets accidentally.

Stop your cat from chasing mice and birds by playing with it more at home. Use toys it can chase.

Did Tibbles Get a Bad Rap?

When Tibbles arrived on Stephens Island, there were probably fewer than 20 of the Stephens Island wrens still there. Tibbles may have killed some of the last of the flightless wrens, but he didn't wipe out the entire species by himself. He wasn't the only pet cat people had brought to Stephens Island, and some had run away from their homes to become wild or feral (see page 51). So maybe the humans who brought the cats to the island should share the blame with Tibbles.

Wildcats

Like Tibbles, all cats are hunters, especially the 38 species of wildcats. The largest of these cats are known as the "big cats." These include jaguars, leopards, lions, and tigers. They're also known as the roaring cats—a lion's roar can be heard 8 kilometers (5 miles) away. But none of these big cats can purr.

The lion is the only cat that lives in a group. The group, called a pride, usually includes five or six related females, their cubs, and one or two males. The top male is the one with the blacker mane. The lion is the only cat with a tuft on the end of its tail, and the male lion is the only cat with a mane.

The world's largest cat is the Bengal tiger. It can be up to 3.1 meters (10 feet) long, about as long as a small car. This big cat can weight up to 258 kilograms (569 pounds), about as much as 60 pet cats. It can hunt prey as large as antelopes and water buffalo. A tiger's stripes are unique, just like human fingerprints. Tigers, along with jaguars and fishing cats, like to swim.

The cheetah is the world's fastest land animal—it can reach speeds of 112 kilometers (70 miles) per hour. Its long tail helps the big cat keep its balance while chasing prey such as gazelles and hares. The cheetah is the only cat that can't retract its claws.

Cats have been blamed for the extinction of 33 species around the world. According to the Smithsonian Conservation Biology Institute, as many as 3.7 billion birds are killed by cats each year. But others point out that millions of birds die naturally as well, from starvation or disease, and that cats tend to catch sick or weak birds.

Actually, 99 percent of animals currently threatened by extinction are at risk because of human activities, says the Center for Biological Diversity in the United States. More than 25 animals become extinct every day according to the World Wildlife Fund. This is nearly 1,000 times the rate of extinction that occurs naturally.

Since humans first came to New Zealand, at least 51 native bird species have become extinct. People need to think carefully about how their activities affect the other animals that share this planet. Once a species becomes extinct, it can never be brought back.

The Tasmanian tiger, or thylacine, became extinct in the 1930s. It was about as big as a large dog and was a marsupial, like a kangaroo.

A cat can leap 2 meters (6.5 feet) high to catch a bird. The hunter's powerful rear legs propel it up into the air. Sharp claws on a cat's front paws help it swat its prey and stun it.

Working Cats

Able Seacat Simon

"**S**imon! Simon! Where are you?"

British Royal Navy sailor George Hickinbottom frantically searched the smoldering wreckage of his ship. At least 25 crew members were dead or dying and many more were injured. So Hickinbottom couldn't spare much time to search for the ship's feline mascot. But where was Simon? Had the cat been blown off the ship?

As he searched, Hickinbottom thought about when he first found Simon in the dockyards of Hong Kong about a year earlier when his ship, the HMS *Amethyst* (HMS stands for "His [or Her] Majesty's Ship"), stopped for supplies. The black-and-white cat was about a year old then, skinny and ill. The young sailor decided to smuggle the kitten on board ship.

The crew of the HMS *Amethyst*—including Simon, of course!

Hickinbottom had tucked Simon into his jacket and stealthily carried him to his tiny cabin. Soon, all the sailors on *Amethyst* were glad Hickinbottom had snuck Simon aboard. The clever cat was an ace at catching and killing rats. The seamen also liked Simon's cheekiness—he left presents of dead rats in sailors' bunks and even liked to curl up for a nap in the captain's gold-braided hat!

Despite this, the captain liked Simon, too. As soon as Simon heard the captain's whistle, the friendly feline would come running from wherever he was on the ship. Simon would trot along with the captain when he did his rounds, checking the ship each night.

The Chinese Civil War, between the nationalist party (Kuomintang) and the Chinese Communists (People's Liberation Army or PLA), had begun in 1927. In April 1949, the *Amethyst* was sailing from the Chinese city of Shanghai up the Yangtze River to Nanking (now called Nanjing).

Crimean Tom

The Crimean War (1853–1856) pitted Russia against countries like England, France, and Turkey. Much of the conflict took place in Crimea, in Eastern Europe. By 1854, the city of Sevastopol in the Crimea was occupied by British and French troops, but they had no food and were starving.

One day, some English soldiers found a friendly cat and brought him back to their base. Tom, as the cat was quickly named, looked healthy and well fed. So the soldiers followed him and he led them to a hidden storeroom of food. Crimean Tom saved the soldiers' lives.

The *Amethyst* was on its way to replace the ship that had been guarding the British embassy there against the Communists. Britain also wanted a ship there in case they needed to evacuate embassy staff.

On April 20, 1949, the Communists opened fire on *Amethyst*. The ship was far enough away that the shots missed, but an hour later, the shooting began again from a new location.

This time, the damage was devastating. The PLA explosive shells hit the bridge, where the ship's steering wheel was located. *Amethyst* drifted onto a mud bank and was stuck, unable to get away. One of the first rounds of shooting also tore through the captain's cabin, where Simon had been sleeping. The captain was dying—had the ship's mascot been hit as well?

Where was Simon?

Despite Simon's white paws, chest, and mouth, the sailors onboard *Amethyst* usually called him "Blackie."

Simon in Danger

When the explosive shell hit the bridge of the *Amethyst*, it blasted a hole in the wall. Simon likely streaked away, but he couldn't outrun the flying metal and shrapnel. The cat's legs and back were badly injured. Even his whiskers were singed off.

When cats are injured, they often crawl into small, dark spaces to be alone, so Simon probably stumbled into a rubble-covered corner and passed out. Just after midnight, the crew managed to get *Amethyst* moving again and sailed it out of range of the guns. Eventually, Petty Officer George Griffiths found Simon, weak, scared, and covered in blood.

By this point, all the wounded humans had been cared for, so the doctor had time to examine Simon. The medical man shook his head gravely. The little cat was wounded in four places. With a sinking heart, the doctor cleaned and stitched up Simon's wounds. The ship's mascot wasn't expected to last long.

Amethyst sailing away from Hong Kong on August 10, 1949. The circle shows the damage to the ship. The discs on the ropes stopped some rats from sneaking on board—but not all.

Meow!

During the Crimean War, Russian soldiers buttoned their coats over their regiments' fluffy kitten mascots to keep themselves warm.

Today's ships still use rat guards on their lines, or ropes, to try to keep rats from creeping aboard.

Meow!

Even ancient Egyptians and Vikings knew the importance of having cats aboard their ships for hunting mice and rats.

Back on Patrol

To everyone's surprise, Simon made it through the night. After he rested for a few days, his wounds began to heal and, slowly and painfully, he began to walk around the ship.

Amethyst was stuck on the river for months because the Communists refused to let it move. Supplies were beginning to run low. While Simon was recovering, rats had gorged themselves on the ship's food supplies and invaded the crew's living quarters, where the rodents could spread diseases.

So Simon took up his rat-catching duties again, catching at least one a day, often more. As well, he began visiting the wounded sailors. The friendly cat helped raise the men's spirits.

Award-winning Mascot

But the situation was getting desperate. So on the night of July 30, 1949, the ship made a desperate dash up the river to the East China Sea. Success! The ship was finally free and safe.

On August 10, the crew received word that Simon would be awarded the Dickin Medal, a prestigious bronze medallion that honors the work of animals in wartime. His fellow sailors gave him the rank of "Able Seaman," which meant Simon was a qualified, experienced sailor.

Amethyst sailed home for England, arriving there in early November. Simon was to be awarded his Dickin Medal on December 11. But on November 27, the cat who had endured such disaster became ill. Despite the best vet care, he died the next morning.

Simon made it back to England from Shanghai, but didn't live long enough to receive his Dickin Medal (right).

World War I Fighting Felines

During World War I (1914–1918), the British army employed 500,000 cats in the trenches, where the soldiers lived and fought. The cats killed rats and detected poison gas. They were also important mascots, helping relieve the stress of battle.

Lieutenant Lekeux of the Belgian army adopted Pitouchi, a mostly white kitten. One day, they were near German lines when enemy soldiers approached. Lekeux lay still—however, he knew he'd been spotted.

Suddenly, Pitouchi jumped up. The Germans shot at him and missed. They then decided they hadn't seen a man after all, but only the cat, and left. Lekeux owed his life to his feline friend.

Feline mascots, like these two kittens, are common on ships. As well as killing mice and rats, cats raise the spirits of the crew.

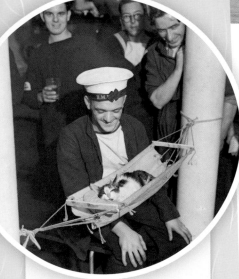

During World War II, Convoy, the cat on the HMS *Hermione*, had his own hammock. The cat was named for the many times he sailed aboard the ship when it was on convoy, or escort, duty.

Unsinkable Sam

Another brave cat aboard a warship was Oscar—at least that was his name when he was on the German battleship *Bismarck* during World War II. When the ship sank on May 27, 1941, most of the crew drowned. But Oscar was picked up by the English destroyer the HMS *Cossack*.

Perhaps Oscar was bad luck because *Cossack* was then torpedoed and sunk on October 24, 1941. However, Oscar was again rescued and sailed to Gibraltar, the British territory at the point where the Mediterranean Sea meets the Atlantic Ocean.

From there, Oscar sailed out on the HMS *Ark Royal*. But less than three weeks later, *that* ship was torpedoed and sunk. Guess who was rescued yet again?

By now, Oscar had a new name: Unsinkable Sam. He was also given a new job—on land, this time. He was made mouse-catcher in the Governor General of Gibraltar's office buildings. His portrait hangs in the National Maritime Museum in Greenwich, England.

Made It by a Whisker

U-boat was another famous British sailing cat in World War II. (In German, a submarine is called an *Unterseeboot*, or "undersea boat," which often is shortened to *U-boot*. U-boat is the English version of this name.) Whenever U-boat's ship reached its port, he would jump ship and not reappear until just before his ship sailed.

One day, U-boat didn't show up and the ship was forced to sail away. The crew was heartbroken at losing its mascot. Then suddenly, they saw a furry streak racing along the dock. U-boat made a daring leap onto the ship, then sat down and washed himself as if nothing had happened. But all the men were glad to have their good-luck charm back.

Great Britain's Most Honored Cat

Many other cats served on ships in World War II and other wars but Simon is still the most famous shipboard cat. Although his ship was able to escape the Chinese Civil War, by 1950, the Communists, the side the British were fighting, had gained control of almost all of mainland China.

In 1975, Britain's Royal Navy banned cats and other pets from all ships for health reasons. Simon was the first—and so far only—cat to win the Dickin Medal. He was the most honored cat in all of Great Britain and he even received an obituary in *Time* magazine.

When sailors had time on their hands while their ship was out at sea, they sometimes taught their mascots to perform tricks. This cat learned how to shake a paw and jump through someone's arms (shown here).

Around the World— and Beyond!

Today, cats still hold important jobs as mousers and ratters, and not just on ships and in trenches. From the world-famous Hermitage Museum in St. Petersburg, Russia, to the British prime minister's home in London, cats are on duty. But cats have lots of other jobs.

Félicette was one of about 14 cats trained by the French space agency to go into space. Her flight lasted 15 minutes and she was recovered safely when her capsule parachuted back down to Earth.

The most out-of-this-world job any cat has ever held is as an astrocat. On October 18, 1963, Félicette was blasted into space by France. She was the first cat in space and provided important information to scientists back on Earth about brain function in outer space.

Lemon is Japan's first police cat. In his blue uniform, he goes on calls with other officers. Since 2012, Lemon has helped put people at ease in interviews— he works especially well with children and elderly people. In 2017, the Bourke Police Station in New South Wales, Australia, adopted an all-black cat whose duties include "chasing mice and assisting officers with their paperwork." His name is PC Splashe— "PC" usually stands for "Police Constable," but in this case it means "Police Cat"!

PC Splashe taking a well-deserved break from fighting crime. The Darling River Police Force Facebook page often features photos of PC Splashe.

Hammer the Hero

In 2003, the 4th Infantry Division of the United States Army entered Iraq. The company known as Team Hammer was the lead element in the push and was often in danger.

So when Staff Sergeant Rick Bousfield spotted a friendly kitten, the little tabby's playful silliness was a welcome relief. The cat, soon named Hammer, headed out on missions with the soldiers and slept in their bunks. During artillery attacks, soldiers tucked Hammer into their body armor to keep him safe.

When the company headed back to the United States in 2004, Bousfield brought Hammer home with him to Colorado.

At the Novorossiysk Library in Russia, Kuzya is an assistant librarian. In Spencer, Iowa, feline Dewey Readmore Books became world famous for cheering up library patrons and staff. Many bookstores also employ cats to chase mice and make the store cozier. The cats like the many places to nap that the stacks of books provide.

Nowadays, many cats "work" at cat cafés. The first one opened in Taipei, Taiwan, in 1998. These coffee shops provide people who can't own cats with a chance to pat a friendly feline. Today, there are cat cafés all over the world, including in Toronto and Vancouver in Canada, and New York City and Orlando, Florida, in the United States. Some of the cats can be adopted.

Meow!

Look online for *The Yangtse Incident*, a 1957 British war movie about HMS *Amethyst*. Simon isn't mentioned in the film, but you'll see a black-and-white cat in some scenes.

The Caturday Cat Café in Ratchathewi, Bangkok, is always busy— sometimes there's a line-up of cat fans waiting to get in. About 40 cats live here, with 20 of them roaming the café at a time.

Spy Cats

Siamese "Bug" Detectors

The two Siamese cats were dozing peacefully in a pool of sunshine on the floor of the embassy. As pets of Henri Helb, the Dutch ambassador to Russia in the early 1960s, they had a good life in the embassy in Moscow. They spent their time curled up together, just lazing about.

So Helb was amazed one day when his napping cats suddenly bounced up and arched their backs as if they'd heard something shocking. The pair of Siamese cats raced to the wall of Helb's office. With their dark paws, they scratched the walls, all the time meowing loudly. Their chocolate-colored noses sniffed the air, while their mahogany ears quivered and twitched.

The staff at the embassy were sure there must be a mouse or rat infestation in the walls. But there was no sign of rodents anywhere.

The ambassador was bewildered. Why did his cats keep waking from their cat naps, clawing at the walls and howling in that peculiar Siamese cat way? Sometimes they'd scratch at one location on the wall, other times they'd paw at different places.

If it wasn't mice or rats disturbing the cats, what could it be? It took a while, but Helb finally realized the cats must be hearing the high-pitched buzz of a microphone (sometimes called a "bug" when used to spy on people) being switched on. The sound was so high that humans couldn't hear it, but the Siamese picked it up, no problem.

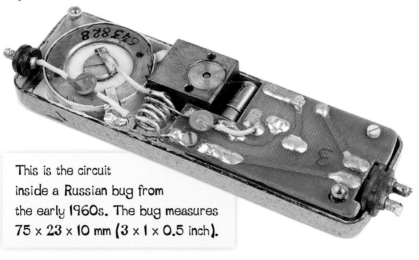

This is the circuit inside a Russian bug from the early 1960s. The bug measures 75 × 23 × 10 mm (3 × 1 × 0.5 inch).

After carefully watching where the cats scratched, the ambassador and his staff figured out there were about 30 microphones in his office. Someone was activating them from a distance using radio waves and recording everything that was said in the study.

From about 1947 to 1991, many countries spied on one another, looking for top-secret information. This period, which grew out of the conditions at the end of World War II, was known as the Cold War and mostly involved the United States (and its allies, including the Netherlands) and Russia (and countries associated with it). It was a tense time because the Cold War often seemed about to turn into a real war.

Ambassador Helb realized that the microphones in his study in Moscow had likely been hidden there by Russian spies—who else had the opportunity to plant the devices? And who else would be so motivated to spy on him?

Helb was faced with a huge dilemma: Now that his Siamese cats had revealed the Dutch embassy was bugged, what should he do about it?

Fur Facts

When a Siamese kitten is born, it's almost all white. As it gets older, a gene that Siamese cats carry dictates that the cooler parts of its body will darken. These are its "extremities"—the parts farthest from the cat's core—and include its ears, paws, and tail. A Siamese's face also darkens because it's cooled by air passing through its nose.

The darker areas on a Siamese are called its "points." And the colder it is where the cat lives, the darker its points will likely be. The same gene that gives these cats their points is also responsible for their blue eyes.

The Savvy Ambassador

Helb was worried that if he protested about the microphones to the Russians, it would cause an incident that could escalate the Cold War and threaten world peace. Besides, he had no proof the microphones had been planted by the Russians.

Instead, Helb and his wife and staff used the microphones to their own advantage. How? Making sure to speak near the hidden microphones, they grumbled about how long it was taking the Russians to repair the sewer outside the embassy. Early the next morning, plumbers arrived to repair the sewer.

Another day, the ambassador's wife was annoyed that the flower bulbs she had ordered from Holland were being delayed by the Russian customs department. She complained loudly to her husband and made sure she was standing close to a wall in his study. The bulbs were delivered the next day.

That proved to Helb that the Russians were listening in on the secret microphones. He decided not to confront them about their spying. But Helb and his staff knew never to discuss any top-secret information near the listening devices.

Siamese cats like lots of attention from their owners and will demand it with their loud, raspy voice. In the case of the Dutch embassy cats, the ambassador was very glad they'd demanded attention and let him know they'd uncovered the undercover microphones.

The story of the Siamese cats' super-sensitive hearing wasn't told until years after the Russian spy ring had been broken.

During the Cold War, people worried that a nuclear bomb might blow up the Earth.

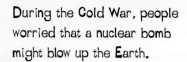

A Siamese cat's ears are large with a wide base and are positioned towards the side of the head.

Meezer

The original Siamese cats had rounder heads and thicker bodies than modern Siamese. Today's long-bodied cat with its triangular head and very long, |thin tail has been specially bred that way since breeders and cat show judges prefer this look.

These cats weren't always as popular as they are now. When the first Siamese cats arrived in Britain in the late 1800s, a reporter described them as "an unnatural nightmare of a cat."

Siamese are well known for meowing a lot. Their loud, low-pitched yowling is known as "meezer," which is the breed's nickname.

Sniffer Spy Cat

Keen senses of smell, hearing, and seeing—cats have them and it makes them great spies. When criminals overfished so much sturgeon in Russia's Caspian Sea that the fish were almost extinct, what did the police do? They hired a sniffer cat to spy on and detect the sturgeon smugglers.

In 2003, police in Stavropol, near the Caspian Sea, got Rusik, a light gray, short-haired cat, on the job. He was incredibly accurate at sniffing out stashes of sturgeon and so led the police to the poachers.

Sadly, it wasn't long before the smugglers were on to Rusik. After just a few months of working as a police cat, he was hit by a car. Some people say it was no accident—Rusik had previously found hidden sturgeon in that very car.

Sturgeon eggs are made into caviar, so are very valuable.

Acoustic Kitty

Scientists have tried to *create* the perfect spy cat. During the 1960s, the Central Intelligence Agency (CIA) in the United States decided it needed a mobile bugging device, a gadget that could actually follow people the CIA wanted to spy on. What could be less suspicious-looking than a cat? So Project Acoustic Kitty was developed to implant cats with listening devices. Scientists took five years to create equipment small enough to be undetectable.

Finally, a cat was trained and implanted with the devices. For its first test, Acoustic Kitty was loaded into a van and dropped off near the Russian embassy. But within seconds, the cat was hit and killed by a taxi. Officials realized this kind of accident could happen to any cat. So Project Acoustic Kitty was shut down—after costing more than $15 million!

Meow!

Siamese don't see well at night. Their eyes lack the tapetum, the part of the eye that amplifies dim light for other cats and gives them good vision at night.

A Siamese cat has a very short coat that lies close to its body, which is another reason why these cats look skinny. Their fur is fine and glossy with no undercoat, unlike most other cats. Siamese shed very little and rarely need to be brushed.

Ragdolls, Pixie-Bobs, and Ocicats

Maine Coon   Persian   Abyssinian   Bengal   Sphynx

Siamese cats are just one of the more than 40 breeds of cats officially recognized at cat shows. The world's most popular breed is the Persian (above, second from left). This snub-nosed breed is famous for its sad or grumpy face, and its fur may be 12.5 centimeters (5 inches) long.

The largest breed of cat in the world, the ragdoll, has beautiful blue eyes. It gets its name because it relaxes completely, like a ragdoll, when it is picked up. The Singapura is the smallest cat breed. It weighs as little as 1.8 kilograms (4 pounds)—the average cat weighs twice that.

Some breeds have unusual coats. For instance, the Turkish Van, from Turkey's Lake Van area, has such a thick coat that it's water resistant. Because of its coat, this breed actually likes swimming. Most cats hate water because it chills them—their fur doesn't insulate well when wet.

The ocicat gets its name because its furry coat is spotted like an ocelot's. This smart, affectionate breed is also known for its long body and long legs.

One of the most unusual breeds is the sphynx (above right), which is hairless. Since it has no fur to absorb its body oil, owners have to bathe these cats. Sphynx kittens are wrinkled all over, while adults have wrinkles just around their heads.

Other breeds have different unusual features. The pixie-bob gets its name because it looks like a wild bobcat. These cats are often polydactyl (right), which means they have more than the usual number of toes. The Scottish fold looks like a teddy bear or owl, thanks to its forward-folding ears and big round head and eyes.

Snooping on Cats

Researchers have turned the tables and spied on cats. In 2013, scientists fitted 50 felines in the British village of Shamley Green with Global Positioning System (GPS) collars and cameras. They wanted to discover what cats do when they're not at home.

The researchers found that almost none of the cats traveled more than 50 meters (165 feet) from home. The cats' activities were affected by weather, feeding times, and their owners' timetables. There were few fights over territory—the cats seemed to "time share" the area.

Infrared cameras on the cats allowed scientists to watch them even in the dark. During the night or day, not many of them hunted birds or mice, preferring canned cat food.

Scientists had already followed lions using **GPS** collars (above). The cats' cameras showed some cats slipping through cat flaps (left) into other cats' homes to sneak snacks!

Meow!

Today, Siamese are one of the most popular breeds in the world. They originated in Thailand, once known as Siam—that's how the cats got their name.

Cats That Help

Dr. Oscar, C.A.T.

and Heal

The nurse held her breath as she watched the large, fluffy cat stalk down the hall of the nursing center. Oscar walked right by one doorway without even stopping. At another, he looked in, but soon continued on his stroll.

When Oscar disappeared into another door, the nurse began walking quickly down the hall toward the room. But before she got very far, the cat was back in the hall and she heaved a sigh of relief.

Oscar patrolled the length of floor, stopping to sniff in a few doorways, sitting down in some, and trotting right by others. When he'd finally checked all the rooms, he leaped up onto a stack of files at the nursing station, closed his big green eyes, and curled up for a nap.

The nurse relaxed. Now that Oscar had done his round and checked all the patients, she knew they'd be safe for the night.

About six months after Oscar the cat arrived at the Steere House Nursing and Rehabilitation Center in 2005, staff noticed he seemed to have a strange ability. It looked as if the gray-and-white tabby could tell when patients were about to die.

Many seniors like cats because they provide love and company. Caring for cats and feeding them are good for older people since these activities help seniors get exercise.

The residence in Providence, Rhode Island, is for people with dementia (an illness that affects the brain) who are near the end of their lives. Patients' deaths are common here and expected.

But staff are nowhere near as precise as Oscar at predicting when the patients will pass away. Once, the staff put Oscar on the bed of a person who they felt was dying because they wanted Oscar to keep him company. Instead, the tabby ran away—and went to sit with a patient in another room. Oscar was right. The second patient passed away that night, while the person the staff thought would die first lived for another two days.

Oscar isn't the kind of cat who craves attention from people. He generally keeps to himself, often ignoring both the patients and the staff. He sometimes even hisses at people if they get too close!

But when someone has just two to four hours of life left, Oscar gently curls up on the patient's bed. He purrs as he lies there and sometimes nudges the person. While he's on the job watching over a dying patient, Oscar stays on the bed almost the entire time. He may slip out to grab a snack, but he's quickly back on guard.

Therapy Cats

Cats trained to provide love and comfort to people in hospices, nursing homes, retirement residences, and schools are known as therapy cats. Studies have shown that when patients interact with cats, they relax and their injuries heal faster.

Therapy cats can be any breed, but they must be friendly, gentle, and patient. They have to enjoy being patted, no matter how clumsily. And they can't be bothered by loud noises or dogs.

Helping children with hearing, language, and speech problems by reducing their fears and relaxing them is just one thing therapy cats can do. They also help stroke victims recover, lower their blood pressure, and ward off depression.

Cat Videos

Being a therapy cat isn't the only way a cat can become famous. Some scientists say people put pictures of their cats online because they want to show off their favorite felines but can't take them on walks.

MY VIDEOS

Related videos

12,574,375 Views

15,574,003 Views

12,574,3475

Happy Cat

Happy Cat is a smiling gray British shorthair whose photo with the caption "I can has cheezburger?" has become famous. It inspired the LOLcat meme on the Internet.

Lil BUB

A toothless cat whose tongue always hangs out is an Internet sensation. Lil BUB has a bone disorder and short legs, so she waddles instead of walks.

Grumpy Cat

A cat named Tardar Sauce has become famous as Grumpy Cat. Her constant grumpy expression is due to her underbite and feline dwarfism. Grumpy Cat has even made a movie.

Maru

Maru is a Scottish fold (see page 70) living in Japan and may be the most famous cat on the Internet. Videos of him playing have been viewed more than 300 million times.

Oscar on the Job

This feline forecaster trots along the halls several times a day, separate from the doctors and nurses making their rounds. Oscar observes and sniffs the patients. He's so accurate in his predictions that if he's found sleeping with a patient, even one the staff feel isn't close to death, the nurses will call the patient's family.

Oscar performs an important service by allowing family members the chance to say goodbye to their dying relative. When the patient passes away, Oscar slips off the bed and quietly pads off down the hall.

If family members are too far away to get to the nursing center before a patient dies, it brings them comfort to know that Oscar was with their relative. Thanks to Oscar, no one has to die alone.

Usually, families are comfortable having Oscar in the room as their loved one passes away. But some families prefer not to have him present. In that case, he marches back and forth in front of the door, sometimes meowing in protest.

Oscar's unique ability to detect dying patients made international headlines after Dr. Dosa published an article about the cat.

Lifesavers

Michael Edmonds of Sheffield, England, suffers epileptic seizures without warning. (Epilepsy is a disease of the nervous system.) There are no symptoms that humans can notice, but his cat, Tee Cee, can detect when a seizure is about to happen. Tee Cee runs to get help and then stays with Edmonds until he regains consciousness.

Mia Jansa (right) owes her life to her cat Pippa. Jansa lives in Kent, England, and has diabetes, a disease that affects the level of sugar in the blood. When Pippa senses that Jansa's blood sugar level has dropped too low, the cat runs to Jansa's mom, who can then give her daughter needed medicine.

Famous Feline

David Dosa, a doctor in the nursing home, wrote a book about Oscar and his incredible ability. *Making the Rounds with Oscar: The Extraordinary Gift of an Ordinary Cat* turned Oscar, a stray adopted from a local animal shelter, into a world-famous celebrity.

Oscar is often mentioned in obituaries by grateful family members who appreciate his care and the comfort he brings. He received an award from Home and Hospice Care of Rhode Island for the work he does in "end-of-life care." As well, look for this perceptive cat on Facebook, where he has his own account.

Meow!

Therapy cats aren't just for adults. They relax kids staying in hospitals, assist children who have developmental disabilities, and help teenagers at juvenile detention centers.

Some days Oscar wants to sit on Dr. David Dosa's lap, and other days Oscar ignores the man who made this cat famous by writing a book about him!

How Does Oscar Do It?

No one knows for sure how the feline predicts patients' deaths. Dr. Dosa says, "The cat might be picking up on specific odors surrounding death." Dr. Joan Teno, another doctor who cares for the residents where Oscar lives, agrees: "I think there are certain chemicals released when someone is dying, and he is smelling and sensing those."

As cells die, the carbohydrates in them break down into chemicals called ketones (KEY-tones). These biochemicals, which have a strong and distinct smell, are released by the dying cells. Some scientists think Oscar may be attracted to this odor.

Veterinarian Dr. Margie Scherk from Vancouver, British Columbia, has this explanation for Oscar's uncanny sense: "Cats can smell a lot of things we can't, and cats can certainly detect illness." Oscar came to the dementia unit as a kitten, and, as Dr. Jill Goldman, an American animal behaviorist, states, he had "ample opportunity . . . to make an association between 'that' smell [and death]."

A cat's sense of smell guides it to prey, tells it if food is edible, and even helps a lost cat find its way home.

Dying people release chemicals known as ketones.

Cat Nurse

Radamenes is a therapy cat with a twist—he helps other animals. He lives at an animal shelter in Bydgoszcz, Poland, where he helps comfort cats and dogs that need surgery or other procedures.

The little black cat was a stray with severe breathing problems when he first came to the shelter. He wasn't expected to live, but when staff heard him purr, they decided to try to save him.

As soon as Radamenes recovered, he began helping the other animals around him. He'll groom them and lie beside them to keep them warm. Staff says he's a full-time nurse!

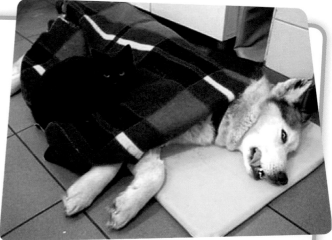

Dr. Oscar's Diagnosis

Some people suggest that Oscar likes to sit with people who are near death because they're often covered with a heated blanket and the furry predictor likes the warmth. Others believe that Oscar picks up on cues from the behavior of the nurses, or perhaps he notices how quiet and motionless the dying patient is. However, none of the other cats in the nursing home have shown the same unusual ability. Oscar has correctly foretold the deaths of more than 100 people at the home. Staff have been keeping records of the cat's predictions and he's rarely wrong.

Dr. Dosa said, "Lots of families have told me that having Oscar around is a great comfort for them and their loved ones. Whether it's just cuddling up to people who are alone or keeping children busy, it's really something that the families were grateful and thankful for."

Therapy cats (see page 75) can help mentally challenged people and patients with cancer feel happier.

Meow!

Cats purr when they're happy and to make themselves feel better. Purring stimulates bones and other tissues to repair themselves.

Time Line

34 million years ago
Proailurus, the first cat ancestor, appears

3.4 million years ago
The ancestor of today's domestic cat first appears

7500
Grave found in Cyprus shows cats were already kept as pets

2000
Egyptians tame wild cats

CE

390
The cat cult is banned as a religious movement in Egypt

1960s
Project Acoustic Kitty attempts to create the first perfect spy cat

early 1960s
Siamese cats detect microphones in Dutch embassy in Moscow

1963
Félicette becomes the first cat in space

1949
Simon wins the Dickin Medal for bravery during the Chinese Civil War

1894
Tibbles the cat arrives on Stephens Island, New Zealand

1859
Inventor Nikola Tesla becomes fascinated with electricity thanks to his cat Mačak

1854
Crimean Tom saves British and French troops in Sevastapol

1000
Vikings take cats on their ships to combat mice and rats

1300s to 1700s
Millions of cats wiped out in Europe because people think they're evil

1620
Pilgrims arrive in North America, bringing with them a distrust of black cats

1852
Earliest written record of the maneki-neko legend

2011
The first picture of Lil BUB is posted to the Web

2012
Radamenes becomes a therapy cat at an animal shelter in Bydgoszcz, Poland

2012
Kuzya begins work at the Novorossiysk Library in Russia

2008
The first video of Maru is uploaded

2007
Videos of Happy Cat hit the Internet

2012
Grumpy Cat first becomes famous

1988
Dewey Readmore Books is left at the library in Spencer, Iowa

2005
Oscar comes to live at the Steere House Nursing and Rehabilitation Center

2012
Lemon becomes Japan's first police cat

1994
DNA from Snowball the cat convicts Douglas Beamish of murder

2004
Tama becomes stationmaster in Japan

2013
Scientists use GPS to study the travel patterns of 50 cats in Shamley Green, England

1997
Ketzel composes *Piece for Piano, Four Paws*

2003
Rusik catches sturgeon smugglers in Stavropol, Russia

2017
Bourke Police Department in New South Wales, Australia, adopts police cat PC Splashe

1998
The first cat café opens in Taipei, Taiwan

Places to Visit

Cat Gods
The British Museum, London, England

Royal Ontario Museum, Toronto, Canada

Museum of Egyptian Antiquities, Cairo, Egypt

Bad Luck Cats
Kuching Cat Museum, Kuching, Sarawak, Malaysia

Cats Museum, Lloret de Mar, Catalonia, Spain

Good Luck Cats
Lucky Cat Museum, Cincinnati, Ohio

Maneki Neko Art Museum, Okayama, Japan

Maneki Neko Museum, Seto, Japan

Inspiring Cats
Nikola Tesla Museum, Belgrade, Serbia

Cats Museum, Kotor, Montenegro

Feline Hunting Machines
Cats Museum and Indoor Zoo, Šiauliai, Lithuania

Lion City Kitty: The Cat Museum, Muses and Mansion Singapore

Working Cats
Imperial War Museum, London, England

Cat cafés in Canada: Guelph, Ontario; Montreal, Quebec; Toronto, Ontario; Vancouver, British Columbia; Winnipeg, Manitoba.

Cat cafés in the United States: New York City, New York; Orlando, Florida; Philadelphia, Pennsylvania; San Diego, California; Washington, DC.

Cat cafés around the world: Auckland, New Zealand; London, England; Paris, France; Tokyo, Japan.

Spy Cats
Moscow Cat Museum, Moscow, Russia

The KattenKabinet, Amsterdam, Netherlands

Cats That Help and Heal
Feline Historical Museum, Alliance, Ohio

The Cat Museum, Ito City, Japan

Main Sources

Cat Gods

Kim Dennis-Bryan. *The Cat Encyclopedia*. New York: Dorling Kindersley Publishing, 2014.

Patrick F. Houlihan. *The Animal World of the Pharaohs*. London: Thames and Hudson, 1996.

Abigail Tucker. *The Lion in the Living Room: How House Cats Tamed Us and Took Over the World*. New York: Simon & Schuster, 2016.

Bad Luck Cats

John Bradshaw. *Cat Sense: How the New Feline Science Can Make You a Better Friend to Your Pet*. New York: Basic Books, 2014.

Harry Oliver. *Black Cats & Four-Leaf Clovers: The Origins of Old Wives' Tales and Superstitions in Our Everyday Lives*. New York: Penguin Group, 2010.

John Seidensticker. *Cats in Question: Smithsonian Answer Book*. Washington, DC: Smithsonian Books, 2004.

Good Luck Cats

Mingei International Museum. *Maneki Neko, Japan's Beckoning Cats: From Talisman to Pop Icon: Mingei International Museum's Billie Moffitt Collection*. San Diego, CA: Mingei International Museum, 2012.

Mieshelle Nagelschneider. *The Cat Whisperer: Why Cats Do What They Do—and How to Get Them to Do What You Want*. New York: Bantam, 2013.

Christine Reiko Yano. *Pink Globalization: Hello Kitty's Trek Across the Pacific*. Durham, NC: Duke University Press, 2013.

Inspiring Cats

W. Bernard Carlson. *Tesla: Inventor of the Electrical Age*. Princeton, NJ: Princeton University Press, 2013.

Bruce Fogle. *Cats*. New York: Dorling Kindersley, 2006.

Marc J. Seifer. *Wizard: The Life and Times of Nikola Tesla: Biography of a Genius*. New York: Citadel Press, 2016.

Feline Hunting Machines

Gerardo Ceballos et al. *The Annihilation of Nature: Human Extinction of Birds and Mammals*. Baltimore: Johns Hopkins University Press, 2015.

Luke Hunter. *Wild Cats of the World*. London: Bloomsbury Natural History, 2015.

Peter P. Marra and Chris Santella. *Cat Wars: The Devastating Consequences of a Cuddly Killer*. Princeton: Princeton University Press, 2016.

Working Cats

Jack Canfield. *Chicken Soup for the Cat Lover's Soul: Stories of Feline Affection, Mystery and Charm*. Deerfield Beach, FL: Health Communications, 2005.

Juliet Gardiner. *The Animals' War: Animals in Wartime from the First World War to the Present Day*. London: Portrait, 2006.

Lisa Rogak. *Cats on the Job: 50 Fabulous Felines Who Purr, Mouse, and Even Sing for Their Supper*. New York: St. Martin's Griffin, 2015.

Spy Cats

Kim Dennis-Bryan. *The Complete Cat Breed Book*. New York: DK Publishing, 2013.

Marjorie McCann Collier. *Siamese Cats: Everything about Acquisition, Care, Nutrition, Behavior, Health Care, and Breeding*. Hauppauge, NY: Barron's, 1992.

Ron Reagan. *Siamese Cats*. Neptune City, NJ: T.F.H. Publications, 1988.

Cats That Help and Heal

David Dosa. *Making the Rounds with Oscar: The Extraordinary Gift of an Ordinary Cat*. New York: Hyperion, 2009.

Pam Johnson-Bennett. *Catwise: America's Favorite Cat Expert Answers Your Cat Behavior Questions*. New York: Penguin Books, 2016.

Jake Page. *Do Cats Hear with Their Feet? Where Cats Come from, What We Know about Them, and What They Think about Us*. New York: Smithsonian Books, 2008.

Further Reading

Cat Gods

Andrew Clements. *Temple Cat*. New York: Clarion Books, 1996.

Keltie Thomas. *Animals That Changed the World*. Toronto: Annick Press, 2010.

Kelly Trumble. *Cat Mummies*. New York: Clarion Books, 1996.

Bad Luck Cats

Katrin Behrend. *Cats*. Hauppauge, NY: Barron's 1999.

Juliet Clutton-Brock. *Cat*. New York: Dorling Kindersley, 2014.

Amanda O'Neill. *Cats*. New York: Kingfisher, 1998.

Good Luck Cats

Wendy Henrichs. *I Am Tama, Lucky Cat: A Japanese Legend*. Atlanta: Peachtree, 2011.

Jinny Johnson. *Cats and Kittens*. Mankato, MN: Black Rabbit Books, 2009.

Susan Lendroth. *Maneki Neko: The Tale of the Beckoning Cat*. Walnut Creek, CA: Shen's Books, 2010.

Koko Nishizuka. *The Beckoning Cat: Based on a Japanese Folktale*. New York: Holiday House, 2009.

Inspiring Cats

Carol Dommermuth-Costa. *Nikola Tesla: A Spark of Genius*. Minneapolis: Lerner Publications Co., 1994.

Monica Kulling. *Zap! Nikola Tesla Takes Charge*. Toronto: Tundra Books, 2016.

Elizabeth Rusch. *Electrical Wizard: How Nikola Tesla Lit Up the World*. Somerville, MA: Candlewick Press, 2013.

Feline Hunting Machines

Maria Mihalik Higgins. *Cats: From Tigers to Tabbies*. New York: Discovery Channel/Crown Publishing, 1998.

Jonathan Sheikh-Miller. *Big Cats*. London: Usborne, 2008.

Seymour Simon. *Big Cats*. New York: HarperCollins, 1991.

Working Cats

Marty Crisp. *Everything Cat: What Kids Really Want to Know About Cats*. Chanhassen, MN: NorthWord Press, 2003.

Vicki Myron. *Dewey: The True Story of a World-Famous Library Cat*. New York: Simon & Schuster, 2010.

Rebecca Stefoff. *Cats*. New York: Benchmark Books, 2004.

Spy Cats

Flavia Capra. *Super Cats!* Vercelli, Italy: White Star Pub., 2012.

Meredith Dash. *Siamese Cats*. Minneapolis, Minnesota: ABDO Kids, 2015.

Phyllis Limbacher Tildes. *Calico's Cousins: Cats from around the World*. Watertown, MA: Charlesbridge, 1999.

Cats That Help and Heal

Elizabeth MacLeod. *Why Do Cats Have Whiskers?* Toronto: Kids Can Press, 2008.

Maureen Webster. *Cat Speak: Revealing Answers to the Strangest Cat Behaviors*. North Mankato, MN: Capstone Press, 2016.

Joan Holub. *Why Do Cats Meow?* New York: Dial Books for Young Readers, 2001.

Image Credits

Every effort has been made to trace copyright holders and to obtain permission for the use of the images in this book. The publisher apologizes for any errors or omissions and would be grateful if notified of any corrections that should be incorporated in future reprints or editions.

Front cover, title page. Juniors Bildarchiv GmbH / Alamy Stock Photo; **Back cover, left** © thadthum / iStockphoto.com; **top right** © Andrey_Kuzmin / Shuttertstock.com; **bottom right** © DenisDore / iStockphoto.com; **fur texture throughout** © Natouche / iStockphoto.com; 3 top © cynoclub / iStockphoto.com; **3 top, sphynx only** © adogslifephoto / iStockphoto.com; **3 middle right** © Alexander Mak / iStockphoto.com; **3 bottom left** © Andrey_Kuzmin / Shuttertstock.com; **3 bottom right** © thadthum / iStockphoto.com; **4 top** © MatViv23 / Shutterstock.com; **4 far left** © Andrey_Kuzmin / Shutterstock.com; **4 bottom** © Keren-S / iStockphoto.com; **5 far right** © Andrey_Kuzmin / Shuttertstock.com; **5 bottom** © Nataliya Kuznetsova / Shutterstock.com.

CAT GODS, 6 main © Bigandt_Photography@ iStockphoto.com; **8** Courtesy of the Metropolitan Museum of Art. Bequest of Mary Anna Palmer Draper, 1915; **9 scene with cat** © bravo1954 / iStockphoto.com, scroll background © forplayday / iStockphoto.com; **10** Courtesy of the Metropolitan Museum of Art. Gift of Florence Blumenthal, 1934; **11 top** North Wind Picture Archives / Alamy Stock Photo; **11 bottom** © TerryJLawrence / iStockphoto.com; **12** The Natural History Museum / Alamy Stock Photo; **13 top** Heritage Image Partnership Ltd / Alamy Stock Photo; **13 bottom** © dk_photos / iStockphoto.com; **14** © Valentyna Chukhlyebova / Shutterstock.com; **15** © Mlorenz / Shutterstock.com.

BAD LUCK CATS, 16 main © Bleshka / Shutterstock.com; **17 inset** Courtesy of the British Library; **18 top** © Esteban De Armas / Shutterstock.com; **18 bottom** © GlobalP / iStockphoto.com; **19 top** Courtesy of the British Library; **19 far right**

and inset Courtesy of the Metropolitan Museum of Art. Fletcher Fund, 1933; **20** © Everett Historical / Shutterstock.com; **21 middle** Digital image courtesy of the Getty's Open Content Program; **21 bottom** © Anatoliy Lukich / Shutterstock.com; **22 top** Courtesy of the Metropolitan Museum of Art. Purchase, Mrs. Vincent Astor and Mrs. Charles Payson Gifts, Harris Brisbane Dick and Rogers Funds, 1972; **22 bottom** photographed by Olha Schedrina / The Natural History Museum. Licensed under the Creative Commons Attribution 4.0 International license; **23** Shchipkova Elena / Shutterstock.com; **24** © Velirina / iStockphoto.com; **25** © 8th.creator / Shutterstock. com.

GOOD LUCK CATS, 26 main Arco Images GmbH / Alamy Stock Photo; **27** Courtesy Library of Congress: reproduction number LC-DIG-jpd-01147; **28 top** Courtesy Library of Congress: reproduction number LC-DIG-jpd-00251; **28 bottom** © thadthum / iStockphoto.com; **29** Lebrecht Music and Arts Photo Library / Alamy Stock Photo; 30 top From The New York Public Library. Image ID 1225610; **30 bottom** © agcuesta / iStockphoto.com; **31** © spxChrome / iStockphoto.com; **32** War Archive / Alamy Stock Photo; **33 top** Arco Images GmbH / Alamy Stock Photo; **33 bottom** Courtesy of the owners of Hamish McHamish's Facebook page; **34 top** © nathanphoto / iStockphoto.com; **34 bottom** © Grigorita Ko / Shutterstock.com; **35 top left** © winhorse / iStockphoto.com; **35 top right** © ES3N / iStockphoto.com.

INSPIRING CATS, 36 main © mcantarero / iStockphoto.com; **37 inset** © Dmitry_Skvortsov / Shutterstock.com; **38 top** © Instants / iStockphoto. com; **38 bottom** © Alina R / Shutterstock.com; **39 top** Hi-Story / Alamy Stock Photo; **39 inset** Courtesy Library of Congress: reproduction number LC-B2-1026-9; **40 top** © TheKoRp / iStockphoto.com; **40 bottom, cat** © Alexander Mak / Shutterstock.com; **40 bottom, spark** © Jcomp / iStockphoto.com; **41** © Taina Sohlman / Shutterstock.com; **42 top** © Stefonlinton / iStockphoto.com;

Index

Index continued

Index continued